THE

SCHOOLMASTER'S TRUNK

CONTAINING

Papers on Home-Life in Tweenit

BY

MRS. A. M. DIAZ

ILLUSTRATED

BOSTON
JAMES R. OSGOOD AND COMPANY
(LATE TICKNOR & FIELDS, AND FIELDS OSGOOD & CO.)
1875

BOSTON:
RAND, AVERY, & CO., STEREOTYPERS AND PRINTERS.

NOTE.

The papers here collected were originally published in "Hearth and Home," under the title of "Papers found in the Schoolmaster's Trunk." They embody observations made from actual life by a teacher residing in a country village. In reproducing them, it was thought best to retain at least a portion of the original title.

A. M. D.

CONTENTS.

THE SCHOOLMASTER'S TRUNK.

I.

THE SLAVES OF THE ROLLING-PIN.

PIES again! Always pies! One, two, three, four, this is the fifth time, within, say, ten days or a fortnight, that, to my knowledge, pies have stood in the way of better things.

First, my hostess, Mrs. Fennel, could not leave to take a ride with me a few mornings ago, because "we are entirely out of — pies." Mrs. Fennel, poor woman, is far from well, and what with husband, grown-up boys, and two small children, not to mention myself as boarder, she has a large family to cook for, and only her daughter Martha to help do the work. That breezy morning-ride would have raised her spirits; it would have put new life into her: but — pies. (This is one time.) Then Miss Martha, who is fond of reading, declined the loan of my library-book the other day on account of having to help her mother make — pies. (Two times.) Last evening she could not run up on the hill to see the sun set, because they were trying to get the meat and apple ready over night for — pies. (Three times.) When poor Mrs. Fennel was taken off her work the other day by one of her frequent

ill-turns, Mrs. Melendy came in with offers of assistance.

"Now I can stay just two hours by the clock," said Mrs. Melendy in her sprightly way; "and what shall I take hold of first? Shall I tidy up the room, read to you, bathe your head, make you some good gruel? Or, else, shall I take hold of the mending, or see to the dinner, or what?"

Mrs. Fennel raised her languid lids, and faintly murmured, "Out of pies."

"Dear me!" cried breezy Mrs. Melendy, "I know what that feeling is well enough; and 'tis a dreadful feeling! Why, I should no more dare to set out a meal's victuals without pie than I should dare to fly! For my husband, he must have his piece o' pie to top off with, whatever's on the table." And the sympathizing sister bared her willing arms, and wrestled womanfully with the rolling-pin, I know not how long.

The fifth time was this morning. While sitting in the room adjoining the kitchen, the doors being open between, I heard Martha ask her mother why they could not take a magazine. "I do long for something to read!" said she; "and all we have is just one newspaper a week."

"Oh! we couldn't get much reading-time," said Mrs. Fennel. "If 'tisn't one thing, 'tis another, and sometimes both. There's your father, now, coming with the raisins. These pies will take about all the forenoon." Miss Martha afterward spoke to her father about the magazine.

"We can't afford to spend money on readin'," he answered, in his usual drawling monotone: "costs a sight to live. Now, if we didn't raise our own pork, we should be hard pushed to git short'nin' for our pies."

Such constant reiteration had made me desperate. I strode to the doorway. "And why *must* we have *pies?*" I demanded in tones of smothered indignation. "Why not bread and butter, with fruits or sauce, instead? Why not drop pies out of the work altogether? Yes, drop them out of the world." Miss Martha was the first to recover from the shock of this startling proposition. "Our men-folks couldn't get along without pies, Mr. McKimber," she said.

"Pie-crust does make a slave of a woman, though," said Mrs. Fennel. "There's nothin' harder than standin' on your feet all the forenoon, rollin' of it out."

"Denno 'bout doin' without pie," drawled Mr. Fennel. "'Pears if bread'n sarse'd be a mighty poor show for somethin' to eat."

"'Twould take off the heft of the cookin'," said Mrs. Fennel thoughtfully; "but" (with a sigh) "you couldn't satisfy the men-folks."

I rushed to my chamber in despair. Pie, then, is one of the household gods in Tweenit. But what can I do about it? Something must be done. Suppose I write an "Appeal to Women," and read it at the sewing-circle, pretending it was taken from a newspaper published in — well, in Alaska, or Australia, or the Orkney Islands. We gentlemen are expected to help along the entertainment in some way.

Hark, now, to the music of the rolling-pin sounding from below! That music shall inspire my

"APPEAL.

"My dear friends, this is an age of inquiry. Can any one tell who first imprisoned our luscious fruits in a paste of grease and flour, baptized the thing with fire, and named it pie? And why is this pie a necessity? That is what confounds me. Mothers of families, hard pressed with work, consume time and strength in endless struggles with the rolling-pin. Fathers of families lengthen their bills to shorten their pies. And all this is to what end? The destruction of health. Every stroke on the board demands strength which is worse than thrown away. Every flake of pastry is so much food which were better left uneaten. And as for the time consumed in this kind of labor, who shall count the hours which are daily rolled away, and chiefly by overburdened women, who complain of 'no time' and 'no constitution'?

"One Saturday forenoon I stood on the hill which commands a view of the village. It was 'baking-day.' Being a clairvoyant, I looked through the roofs of the houses, and saw in every kitchen a weary woman, 'standin' on her feet,' rolling, rolling, rolling. Close around some stood their own little children, tugging at their skirts, pleading for that time and attention which rightfully belonged to them. One frail, delicate woman was actually obliged to lie down and rest twice before her task was ended. Another, the mother of an infant not many months old, accomplished hers with one foot on the cradle-rocker.

"We read of despotic countries where galley-slaves were chained to the oar. They, however, after serving their time, went free. Alas for poor woman chained to the rolling-pin! Her sentence is for life.

"We read, too, in ancient story of powerful *genii*, whose control over their slaves was absolute; but this terrible *genius* of the household exacts from its slaves an equally prompt obedience. Is there one among them who dares assert her freedom?

"No: their doom is inevitable. Woman is fore-ordained to roll her life away. Is there no escape? No escape The rolling-board is planted squarely in the path of every little daughter; and sooner or later, if her life be spared, she will walk up to it. May we not call it an altar upon which human sacrifices are performed daily?

"I observed, on the morning just mentioned, that, in the intervals of pastry-making, the *genius of the long-handled spoon* took control, demanding its customary tribute of eggs, sugar, fat, spices, &c., demanding, also, the usual outlay of time and strength which goes to the compounding of cakes; and thus, with rolling, beating, and stirring, the forenoon wore away, leaving in each house its accumulation of unwholesome food.

"You *do* know, madam, that plain living is better for your children? You *would* like more time to devote to them, or for books, or for recreation? Then, pray, why not change all this? Is palate forever to rank above brain? Change your creed. Say, 'I believe in health, in books, in out-doors.' Why don't you *rise*, slaves? Now is your time. Now, when slaves everywhere are demanding their freedom, demand yours.

"*Company?* Thanks for teaching me that word. The kind hospitality of this social little village of Tweenit enables me to be 'company' myself very frequently. And I am aware that much time is spent in the preparation of viands to set before me, which, for variety and richness, could not be excelled. Shall I add, that whenever, at the bountifully-spread tea-tables, I have attempted to start a rational conversation, the attempt usually has been a failure? Books, public men, public measures, new ideas, new inventions, new discoveries, what is doing for the elevation of women,—on none of these subjects had my entertainers a word to offer. Their talk was, almost without exception, trivial, not to say gossipy.

"Therefore, as a member of that institution, which, as everybody says, 'makes a sight of work,' namely, 'company,' I protest. I petition for less variety in food, and more culture. And your petitioner further prays, that some of the spices and good things be left out in cooking, and put into the conversation.

"But the 'men-folks'? Ah, to be sure! Perhaps, after all, it is they who need an appeal."

she must keep her *mind* on her work. And, truly, the calculating and contriving demanded by each day's operations require some mind.

Now, I had the idea, before I was awakened by Mrs. Melendy's remark, that woman's work was not of much account, — just a simple matter of "puttering" about the house. The tempting food which Mrs. Fennel serves up daily stood for a very small part of the labor which it actually represents. And, but for that remark, I might have gone on eating the delicacies spread before me with no more sense of their cost than if they grew on trees, and were shaken down at meal-times. Since my eyes have been opened, however, those delicacies taste too strong of the toil to be relishable; for I see that the rows of pies on the buttery shelves, the mounds of cake, the stacks of doughnuts, do not come there by any magical "sleight o' hand," but are wrought out of the very life of poor Mrs. Fennel, — literally, of her very life. This is not an overstatement, since it is plain to be seen that each day's labor makes demands which her strength is unable to meet. I have observed the languid way in which she drags herself about the house, now and then dropping upon a chair; have noted, at times, — at "hurried" times, — the worn, weary, "all-gone" expression of her face; and have heard her take, oh! very often, those "long breaths," which are sure signs of a wearing-out.

Yes, the poor woman is killing herself with over-work. And when she rests, at last, beneath the turf, people will speak of the mysterious Providence which removed a wife and mother in the midst of her usefulness.

It is about time, one would think, to put a stop to this woman-killing. A harsh phrase? It is not more harsh than the truth; for, if lightening labor will prolong life, insisting upon unnecessary labor is not far removed from that crime. And this unnecessary labor is insisted upon in one way or another.

For instance, I have Mrs. Fennel's own word for it, that pies are "the heft of the cooking;" have heard her speak of rolling out pastry until she was "ready to drop," of beating cake until her arms "hadn't one mite of strength left in them." Yet, to any suggestion that these and other superfluities be omitted, the answer has invariably been, that "the men-folks wouldn't be satisfied without them."

Mr. Fennel is a very good man; and the boys — young men of eighteen and twenty — are very good boys. If the direct question were asked Mr. Fennel, which he most values, his wife's life, or the nice things she prepares for the table, he would answer with horror, if he answered at all, the former. In reality, however, he answers the latter. It is the same with the boys. The men-folks can't eat cold bread; therefore bisuits are rolled out, cut out, and baked, both morning and night; the men-folks make dependence on their cake; the men-folks must have their "piece o' pie to top off with;" the men-folks like to have a pot of doughnuts to go to.

Now, all these things may gratify the palate; but the point is, are they worth the price that is paid for them? I confess that it fairly makes me shudder, sometimes, to see those strong men sit down at table, and, with appetites sharpened by out-of-door exercise, sweep off so unthinkingly and unthankingly the results of Mrs. Fennel's long and weary toil. Do they not *taste something* in those delicacies? detect a flavoring that was never set down in any grocer's bill? They probably do not. Long habit has so accustomed them to the flavor of this *essence of life*, this compound extract of backache, headache, exhaustion, prostration, palpitation, that they do not notice its presence. It would be well for them to do so, however; for it is a terribly expensive article.

Oh, no! they don't taste any thing but what may be bought at the grocer's, or raised on the farm. If they did, if the cost of all these dainties were once made clear to our kind-hearted men-folks, they would not only be satisfied without them, but would beg Mrs. Fennel to stop cooking them; for neither Mr. Fennel nor the boys are wanting in affection for her. Whenever, by overwork, she becomes alarmingly ill, they are ready to harness the horse, and go seven miles for the doctor at any time of day or night. Mr. Fennel never spends his money so freely as in medicine for his wife; and the boys seldom come home from the pastures without bringing her mullein, or some kind of herb, to dry. "So thoughtful of them!" the dear woman remarks with moistened eyes, and cheeks faintly flushed. If they could only be so thoughtful as to consider that rest is better for her than herbs!

All women are not as feeble as Mrs. Fennel? This is true; yet she represents a large class, and one which is rapidly increasing. Mothers of families calling themselves well and strong are hard to find. They too commonly either break down and die, or break down and live. Go into almost any town, any country village even, where pure air and other conditions of health abound, and mark in the sharpened, worn, pinched faces of its elderly women, the effects of overwork and unwholesome food.

Work is necessary. I believe in it; believe in eating too, and in eating what "tastes good," as the phrase is. But to a person of healthy appetite plain food "tastes good," and "topping off" is quite unnecessary. The words "topping off" express the exact truth: implying, that, when the stomach is already full, something is put on the top. (By the way, it is doing this, unless the something be very simple, which spoils the appetite for the next meal.)

No: far be it from me to scorn the pleasures of the palate. I would by no means consider it wicked to eat, semi-occasionally, a bit of cake;

and there may be times in the year when even pie would be in order. But I protest against making these things the essentials; against its being taken for granted, that in whatever press for time, — in sickness and in health, in strength and in weakness, in sorrow and in joy, — the table must be spread with this prescribed, though needless, variety of food.

And, as it is the men-folks who are to "be satisfied," I appeal to them to "be satisfied" with that which requires less of woman's labor and of woman's life.

III.

CONCERNING COMMON THINGS.

WHOEVER would be tranquil, let him not investigate. Ever since I began inquiring into household affairs, my mind has been disturbed by a doubt — not quite a doubt; call it an uneasiness — as to the mental superiority of the dominant sex. No, it cannot amount to positive doubting. That would be to fly in the face of facts. History proves that the greatest philosophers, the greatest artists, the greatest writers, the greatest thinkers, have been men. If woman has the ability to be as great in these directions, why has she not been as great? There has certainly been time enough, — six thousand years at the lowest calculation.

Well, then, since facts cannot be disputed, there can be no reasonable doubt upon this subject; but — No, I won't say *but:* I won't admit the possibility of a *but.* I will only say that it is very puzzling and very annoying to have one's daily observations tend to undermine — not undermine, conflict with — one's belief. And it may happen, that, if a man watch too closely what goes on in doors, the idea will be suggested to him, that while he prides himself, very likely, on working well at one trade, a woman may work well at half a dozen, and not pride herself at all.

Mr. Fennel is a carpenter. Mr. Melendy is a shoemaker. Each is master of one trade, and only one, and works at that all day. Mr. Fennel doesn't stop to mend his shoes. Mr. Melendy doesn't leave off pegging to make a new front-door.

Mrs. Fennel is mistress of many trades. Mrs. Fennel is cook, tailoress, dressmaker, milliner, dyer, housemaid, doctor, and boy's capmaker; also, at times, schoolmaster, lawyer, and minister. For she hears the children's lessons; she adjusts their quarrels with the judgment of a judge; and she gives them sermons on morals which contain the gist of the whole matter.

Of all these occupations, cooking, I observe, ranks the highest. That is sure of attention: the others take their chance. That is cut out of the whole cloth: the others get the odds and ends. I have observed also, in this connection, that the day in doors resolves itself into three grand crises, called the three meals. It is surprising, it is really wonderful, the way these are brought about with every thing else going on beside. Indeed, this prying into domestic affairs has made me surprised twice. First, at the amount of physical labor a woman has to perform; second, that she can carry so many things on her mind at one time, or rather that her mind can act in so many directions at one time, and so quickly. This in-doors work seems commonplace enough; to the fastidious, repugnant even. The same may be said of a mud-puddle. But dip up a dipperful of the mud, examine it closely, and you will find it teeming with life. So, examine an hourful of household work, and you will find it all alive with plans, contrivances, forethoughts, afterthoughts, happy thoughts, and countless trifling experiences, minute, it may be, but full of animation. The puddle is often set in commotion by a passing breeze, or by a stone dropping in. Well, household work, too, has its breezes of hurry and flurry, besides its regular trade-winds, which blow morning, noon, and night. And, if company unexpected isn't like the stone dropping in, then what is it like?

This is written, as the scientific people say, from

observations taken on the spot. One day I spent an hour in watching Mrs. Fennel at her work, and an hour in watching Mr. Fennel at his. Being in a humorous as well as a scientific frame of mind, I played they were my specimens, and that the matter under consideration really did belong to some branch of science, unknown, of course, to a country schoolmaster. I copy from my note-book: —

"Time, forenoon; place, kitchen.

"Fly, my pencil, fly, like Mrs. Fennel's feet! Dinner is getting. It seems now as if every moment were a crisis. What's that she is dropping into hot water? Oh! turnip, sliced and peeled. Meat, pudding, potatoes, squash, beans, &c., require, I see, different lengths of time in the cooking. But they must be on the table at twelve o'clock, done just right; some of them mashed, and all of them hot. Think of the calculation necessary to bring this about! Meanwhile, in the intervals of lifting the pot-lid, Gussy's new suit is being "cut out of old." And here, again, calculation — that is, *mind* — is required in cutting the cloth to advantage.

"Now Mrs. Fennel drops down to take a long breath. 'How much sugar must be put into this gooseberry pie?' Martha asks. 'Rising one cupful.' Now a little girl comes of an errand: 'Mother wants you to write down how to make corn-starch gruel. Bobby's sick.' Mrs. Fennel writes directions. Now she is ironing. Why not wait till after dinner? Oh, to be sure! 'We must iron while we have a fire.' Now Gussy rushes in pell-mell to ask if when he carries Emma's gooseberries for her because she

asked him to, and then stubs his toe, and spills 'em, *he* ought to pick 'em up? Now comes Emma, to say that Gussy tried to stub his toe, because she picked more gooseberries than *he* did when *he* went. Mrs. Fennel adjusts the quarrel; preaches a sermon on envy, truth, and brotherly love; informs Gussy what Malaga is famous for; tries on his jacket (telling a story to make him stand still); catches up a rent in Emma's dress; trades with a tin-peddler (*mind*

3

again); and through all this keeps her eye on the cook-stove; drops things into hot water; forks things out of hot water; contrives places for saucepans, spiders; runs round with a long-handled spoon, now with a knife, stirring, mashing, seasoning, tasting, till at last the moment arrives, and the men-folks arrive, and the grand crisis of the day is at its climax. But oh the flurry and excitement of the last fifteen minutes! the watching the clock, the looking in at the oven, the disappointment when things that should have risen have fallen! As if this did not happen in life always!"

The second hour gave less striking results. I found Mr. Fennel planing and grooving boards. His movements were distinguished by an entire calmness. There was no hurry, no excitement, to keep his mind on the snap every moment; no grand climax for which boards, laths, shingles, nails, and clapboards must be got ready, let come what would. "Too monotonous," the notes read, "to be of any special interest." Had he dropped his plane for a trowel, the trowel for a paint-brush, paint-brush for a whitewash-brush, whitewash-brush for a hod of bricks, or been called upon to slack lime, mix paint, or to give directions for building a hen-house, the proceedings in the work-shop would no doubt have been as entertaining as those in the kitchen. But, as far as hinderances were concerned, Mr. Fennel might have shoved that plane till doomsday, and with a temper smooth and even as his own boards.

Since that time I have observed carefully other men and other women at their work; and thus far my observations show that the average mother of a family requires and uses, in the performance of her daily duties, higher qualities of mind than does the average father of a family in the performance of his. Indeed, the more closely I observe, the more amazed am I at the skill, tact, energy, insight, foresight, judgment, ability, genius, I may almost say, so often displayed by the former.

Well, and what then? Why, then the question arises, "Is woman, in the present condition of things, making the best use of all these high qualities?" This question is not suggested by the fact of her giving herself up so entirely to her family. Oh, no! most emphatically no. Children must have their mother. She belongs to them. The best a woman has, the best an arch-angel has, is none too good for the children. No: the question is suggested, partly by the "observations" I have been making, and partly by the recollection of Mrs. Melendy's remark, that the "three meals take about all day." I am glad the sewing-circle meets here this week; for, by attending to the conversation, I may learn upon what subjects the minds of at least some fifteen or twenty women chiefly dwell.

Another question, and a startling one too, is this: "If woman ever has a chance properly to develop these remarkable qualities of mind, what is going to become of the mental superiority of the dominant sex?"

No more, no more! My brain is confused, my soul disquieted within me. Whoever would be tranquil, let him not investigate.

IV.

THE SEWING-CIRCLE.—HOW IT WAS STARTED.

THE sewing-circle is in session in the adjoining room. It counts thirty-two members in all, — a goodly number for a population of only twenty-five or thirty families. The gathering to-day is not large; a thunder-storm, and a circus at Elmbridge, conspiring to keep many away.

Mrs. Fennel has been telling me about this sewing-circle, and what it is trying, or rather is determined, to do. The people of Tweenit village never had a meeting-house, but have held religious services in the schoolhouse. Now the women want to change all this. They want to build a chapel; and for that purpose they mean to raise eight hundred dollars.

"Eight hundred dollars!" I exclaimed when Mrs. Fennel named the sum. "Why, there's hardly as much money in the place!"

"That's just what the men told us," she answered; "but we have faith."

"I should think so," said I, "and works too."

The men, it seems, threw cold water at the very beginning.

"Where's all that money coming from?" "Lumber high!" "Labor high!" "Saddle the place with debt!" "All nonsense! The old schoolhouse is good enough!"

And the idea might have been quenched entirely, but for the burning zeal of two unmarried women, — "Nanny Joe" and "Nanny Moses," the daughters respectively of Mr. Joseph Payne and Mr. Moses Payne. They believed in a chapel. They preached this belief; and many women were converted. The first convert was Miss Janet (Mr. William Melendy's wife, called "Miss Janet," to distinguish her from four other Mrs. Melendys). A meeting was called at her house. Before its close, the wildest enthusiasm prevailed. The men's objections first were shown up to be scarecrows, then pelted down with ridicule. A sewing-circle was formed, which met once a week to sew "slop-work," and knit toes of stockings, — heels, too, I think. Oh, yes! "heeled and toed:" that's the very expression. In other respects, the stockings were woven. The circle meant business. Some members met early in the morning, and worked all day. Ellinor Payne, who is employed in a tailor's shop at Piper's Mills, gave fifteen dollars of her own earnings. The enthusiasm increased. Did any waver in the faith, influenced by doubting men, Nanny Joe and Nanny Moses were ready to encourage and sustain. Nanny Joe and Nanny Moses were eloquent to persuade, ingenious to devise, skilful to contrive, and untiring in their labors. They fired the ambition of every woman in the place. They took that chapel (the chapel that was to be), and resolved it into its constituent parts, — its doors, windows, timbers, boards, nails even, and induced different individuals to be responsible for, say, a bundle of shingles, a window, a door, a stick of timber. Young and old caught the fever. Little girls vied with each other in earning panes of glass. Blooming maidens took upon their shoulders clapboards, laths, and kegs of nails. Matrons bore bravely their respective burdens of beams, rafters, and flooring; and one cheerful old grandame, a steadfast knitter, smiled under the weight of the desk.

The little girls earned their money by running of errands, and picking huckleberries, and making patchwork cradle-quilts to sell. The older ones also picked huckleberries. When the season was at its height, the circle met in the pastures, and picked its pecks and its bushels. The berries were sent to Piper's Mills to be sold. If there were no other way of sending them, Nanny Joe and Nanny Moses would take Mr. David's old red horse and go themselves. Mr. David Melendy committed himself at the very beginning, by a promise, which, though made in jest, was claimed in terrible earnest, as the old man found to his cost.

"I'll agree to find horse and cart to cart all the work they'll get," said Mr. David sarcastically, when he first heard of the sewing-circle. His narrow vision took in Tweenit village only, where each family generally does its own needlework. But there were eyes of a wider range, — far-seeing eyes, which saw the "store" at Piper's Mills, whereat were left weekly, by an agent from the city, huge bundles of slop-work and stocking-work for the sewers and knitters of that neighborhood. The sewing-circle obtained one of these bundles, and did its work so well that the agent not only promised it more bundles, but heaped bundles upon it; so that Nanny Joe had frequent opportunities of going to Mr. David, and saying, with a mischievous twinkle of her laughing black eyes, "More work to cart, Mr. Melendy!"

"Wal, wal, Nancy," that victim of his own jest

would reply, "I'll stan' by my word. But you must help me ketch him."

This is not so very difficult a task; for that fat old horse of his would as soon be caught as not to be. Whether he goes or stands still is all one to him, and nearly so to his driver. For calmness, for meekness, for sublime indifference, Mr. David's

animal would take the medal. As may be imagined, he is a very *even* horse to drive; never allows himself to be disturbed by outside influences, but jogs heavily on, with a flop and a plunge, unmoved by word or blow.

"Speak of the ancient Nicholas," says the proverb, "and you will see his horns." And, in confirmation of it, behold this identical animal now approaching the house, shaking all over at every flop, as if he were a horse of jelly. Nanny Joe and Nanny Moses have just driven from Piper's Mills with some bundles of work. Nanny Moses holds up a letter. Her fair, round face reminds me of Mrs. Fennel's favorite expression, "Smiling as a basket of chips." Thirty-seven or thirty-eight they say is her age. They also say that she holds her own pretty well, which is saying a good deal; for "her own" must weigh a hundred and fifty, at the least. Anybody might know those two would be intimate, they are so unlike. Nanny Joe is tall, slender; has coal-black hair, coal-black eyes, a sallow complexion, and a chin unnecessarily long. She is pleasing and sprightly; her friend, pleasing and quiet.

Now joyful shouts uprise. There is money in the letter. David Melendy, junior, has sent twenty dollars. These women leave no stone unturned. A few months ago, one of them, while on a visit to the city, called upon all Tweenit-born individuals there residing, and by appealing to their pride, their generosity, or their piety, as suited each case, obtained various sums to help the cause along. Tweenitites dwelling afar, amid Sitka's snows or California's golden sands, were appealed to through the United-States mail; and the letter just received is in answer to one of those appeals. It comes from Sitka; and Nanny Joe says the money is the profits arising from a rise in white bears. I was present the other day at the reading of a letter addressed to one Mr. Ezra Fennel, which must stir the depths of Mr. Ezra Fennel's heart, if not of his pocket-book. Men's money, after all? Well, so is the gold in a gold-mine the gold-mine's gold. There is a great deal in knowing how to work a mine, and a great deal in knowing how to work a pocket-book.

Now that the Sitka excitement is over, and the circle is subsiding into its natural state, I will take a few notes of the conversation. They may throw some light on the subject of my present inquiries. Woman, I perceive, displays mind enough, both at home and abroad; and now I want to find out upon what kind of subjects her mind ordinarily dwells.

V.

NOTES TAKEN AT THE SEWING-CIRCLE.

NOT as a listener, but as an investigator, investigating the very important subject of domestic affairs. Why not call it a scientific subject? Why not found a small science of my own here in this out-of-the-way place? The wise ones, the ones that own the big sciences, won't know any thing about it; and, if they do, they won't try to get mine away from me, having so many heavenly bodies, motive-powers, the forces of Nature, and, in fact, all created things, to attend to.

My science has the forces of Nature in it too (human nature), and a motive-power. Their motive powers act on machinery; mine acts on human beings. It is the power by which woman "carries on the family;" and I have seen for myself that there is a "power of it" used in some families; also that it can be *turned on*, as the factory people say, in other directions; in that of chapel-building, for instance. Give it a name; call it mind-power; for it is a combination of some of the highest mental qualities. Not fully developed, though; oh, no! scarcely begun to be developed yet.

It being settled, then, that woman does possess this motive-power which belongs to *my* science, and which I have named mind-power, the question next arises, Is she doing all she can with it? Is none of it running to waste? What ideas, apart from household affairs, take up her mind mostly? It was to obtain light on this last question, that I resolved to pay attention to the talk at the sewing-circle. I wished to take the level, the mental level, of its members. Their conversation, by revealing what subjects chiefly occupy woman's thoughts, I believed, would give me some idea of how much she is accomplishing with this mind-power of hers.

True, Tweenit is only one village; but it is, probably, much like other villages, and its sewing-circle like other sewing-circles.

NOTES OF CONVERSATION.

Aunt Jinny under the Hill. — Aunt Jinny Piper. Destitute old woman. Much given to rheumatism. Mainly dependent on charity. Might make things go further. No calculation. Slack. Cloth given her not cut to advantage. Mouldy bread in her cupboard. Wore an apron forenoons good enough to wear afternoons. Used white pocket handkerchiefs: why not a square piece of old calico? Grandchild visits her too often. *They say* she *makes* her rheumatism.

AUNT JINNY DOWN AT THE CRICK. — Another Aunt

Jinny Piper. Unmarried. Well off. Chests full of sheets and pillow-cases. Stingy. Got enough of every thing. Might clothe Aunt Jinny under the hill just as well as not. Ought to give land to build chapel on. Great for beating down prices. Paid man that spaded up her garden in pumpkins. Pumpkins overran two cents: told man he must bring back the skins and insides for her pig, to make it all square.

Planning. — "Forecasting" your work. Lying awake nights to plan how next day's baking shall be worked in between the ironing or house-cleaning. Babies make it so you can't carry out your plans. Best not to take much notice of young children, so they'll bear "turning off."

Mis Susan. — Mis Susan, wife of Mr. Henry Melendy. Lives in Pickerel Brook neighborhood. Has traded shawls with a peddler, and got a green one. Don't see what Mis Susan wants of a green shawl. Shouldn't think 'twould be becoming to her. Her shawl was a beautiful shawl. Hadn't had it a great while. Guess she'll be sorry. Don't believe this one's all wool.

Spring o' the Year. — Always want something sour in the spring o' the year. Man that brings along "Archangel Bitters" to sell. Some say your gall runs into your liver; more likely your liver runs into your gall. How does anybody know? Dread spring o' the year. Brings so much work! Nothing to make pies of. Feel lost without pies. Vinegar mince-pies better'n no mince-pies. Soak your cracker in your vinegar. Chop your raisins. Makes beautiful pies, if you take pains. What *my* husband likes, and what *my* husband likes. Children ditto. My Ella B. won't touch molasses gingerbread. My Tommy'll eat his weight in it. My Abner could sit up all night to eat sausage-meat. Sight o' work to make sausage-meat. Sight o' work to cook calf's head. Wants "good sweet pork" with it. Calves' brains make beautiful sauce. (Various recipes omitted.)

Henry T. — Henry T. Rogers. Young man. Began business in the city, and failed. Henry T. always held his head up high. Would have to come down. High-strung all that family were. *They say* he has bad habits. *They say* extravagance did it. *They say* (remainder in whispers).

Fred and Marion. — A pair of lovers. *They say* they've broken off. *They say* she's written him a letter. *They say* he goes with another girl. Dreadful thing to Marion. Probably wear her into a consumption. *They say* she cries all night. 'Course she'll send back his presents. Gold ring, worth how much? Some of his presents worn out, Wonder how his father's property'll be divided.

Fennel Payne and Adeline. — Fennel Payne, a young married man, distantly related to the Fennels and the Paynes. Has wife (Adeline) and small child. Adeline stuck up. Always was stuck up. Has strange notions. Both of 'em have strange notions. Spent five dollars for a picture. No great things of a picture. Adeline sits down to read in the daytime. They go to take walks together. Go up on the hill and sit down sometimes. Funny actions for married folks.

HOW ARE YOU GOING TO HAVE YOUR DRESS MADE?—(Notes omitted. Reason, unfamiliarity with terms used.)

The above is a small part of what was taken down in my note-book.

Summary of observations made up to date in Tweenit Village:—

First, that woman works hard physically, works very hard, and with not much respite.

Second, that in "carrying on the family" (this is a very common phrase here),—in "carrying on the family," and in various ways, she displays mental qualities of a high order.

Third, that in working so hard, or in as far as she works so hard, merely to gratify the palate, she is spending herself physically for an unworthy end.

Fourth, that her mind-power is running to waste in the same direction; also in other directions, as is shown by the not very high tone of her conversation.

VI.

PEBBLES, OR DIAMONDS?

I "DREAMED a dream that was not all a dream," — dreamed of seeing a vast company of women, a multitude whom no man could number, all earnestly engaged in picking up — pebbles. Gems of priceless value lay scattered everywhere around; but these were passed by unnoticed. "Foolish creatures! Why don't they leave the pebbles, and take the diamonds?" I cried.

There was a reason for my dreaming such a dream. I went to Piper's Mills the other day, to carry a bundle of "circle-work" for Nanny Joe. I took Mr. David's horse, and, while there, called on an acquaintance of mine, — Mrs. Royal. A couple of her neighbors had dropped in to tea that afternoon; and I was cordially invited to stay.

"If you don't mind being the only gentleman," said Mrs. Royal. I replied most gallantly that it would give me the greatest pleasure to be placed in so enviable a minority; all the while saying to myself most "scientifically," *Three new specimens. Observe mental habits. Compare with those of sewing-circle members. More light on domestic science. (My science has a name now.)*

I knew something of Mrs. Royal and her friends; and that they differed in many respects from the majority of women. When, therefore, the tea-table talk began, I prepared to listen with interest, believing that my new specimens, though of the same class as my Tweenit friends, — that is, neither poorer nor richer, — would prove to be a different species.

The talk ran first on

TEA-ROSES. — So fragrant! so beautiful! Beautiful? Why, the beauty of even one half-opened bud was too much to take in. Article in the newspapers speaking of a beauty which makes "sense ache." Damask-roses going out of fashion. Wild roses in June reddening the wayside banks. Fragrance of the sweet-brier, of the trailing arbutus. Flowers of spring, and their haunts. Pleasure of giving and of receiving flowers.

ANECDOTES OF THE FLOWER-MISSIONS IN THE CITIES. — Beautiful "mission," that of sending flowers to the sick-beds of the poor. What is being done in various places for the poor, the ignorant, the degraded, and the friendless. It is beginning to be understood that we are all of one family. Will the time ever come when this family feeling shall unite the nations?

THE WAR-SPIRIT. — How shall it be done away? Influence of battle-pictures and battle-stories on the young. Some of the principal studies in schools and colleges are histories of battles. Pictures of military commanders in almost every house. How does all this affect the coming of the time when swords shall be beaten into ploughshares?

IMPORTANCE OF BRINGING GOOD INFLUENCES TO BEAR ON CHILDREN. — Obedience from children. How to secure it, and at the same time encourage in them a proper degree of self-reliance. Best ways of developing the good that is in children. Educating the heart as well as the head. Importance of physical health. When children, as they grow up, "go wrong," who is responsible?

ALLEN WENTWORTH. — A young man who "went wrong." Dissipated. Inherited love of drink. Is it for us who inherited no such tendency to condemn him? Mental and moral qualities handed down. Shall the "born good" despise the "born bad"? Allen Wentworth like character in a novel recently read by one of the company. Other novels and other characters spoken of.

Books and Authors Generally. — Funny scenes recounted and laughed at. Heroes and heroines discussed. Beautiful passages quoted.

Descriptions of Natural Scenery — Woods in spring. In fall. Shadows on the grass. Waving of corn and grain. Sunsets. Sunrises.

We remained together for three or four hours, during which time I took notes, mentally, of the ideas expressed by different members of the company. I have put these notes upon paper in such a way as to show pretty nearly the course of the conversation, and how naturally one thing led to another.

During my ride home I had ample opportunity, thanks to the peculiar temperament of Mr. David's horse, of comparing this conversation with that to which I had listened at the sewing-circle. And what a difference! Why, that first one was so trivial, so aimless, with its never-ending gossip, I actually felt myself growing smaller while hearing it.

And I could but compare the two ways in which the two sets of talkers handled the same subjects. For instance, "spring o' the year" was mentioned by the first merely as a time of house-cleaning, and a dearth of pie-material. The second talked of spring flowers and spring birds, of leaves bursting, and swamps awaking. Children were discussed by the first set, chiefly, I think, with regard to what they liked to eat, or to whether, individually, they were or were not "hard on their clothes;" at any rate, there was no interchange of ideas concerning the right way of bringing them up. The second spoke of children as immortal beings, the training of whom called for a mother's best endeavors. Even in talking about their neighbors there was a difference. Many members of the sewing-circle seemed rather to enjoy the downfall of Henry T., — some even to exult over it. Allen Wentworth, on the contrary, was tenderly spoken of by Mrs. Royal and her friends; and the causes of his wrong-doing were thoughtfully considered.

Then, again, there was a difference in the kinds of enjoyment with which the two sets of people enjoyed their conversations; that of the last being infinitely higher. "How charming!" "Now, isn't that grand!" "What a beautiful idea!" they exclaimed, now and then, as some heart-stirring passage was repeated. The face of each listener or speaker would light up with pleasure; and the eyes would tell that her very soul was enjoying itself. I could but remember, then, Adeline, Fennel Payne's wife, who was blamed by some of the circle for "sitting down to read in the daytime;" as if daytime were only made for rolling out pastry, sewing dresses, and the like. And when that tea-table talk ran on flowers and birds, woods, waters, glorious sunsets, and all the wonderful "out-doors," I again remembered Fennel Payne and Adeline, and how they had been ridiculed for "taking walks," and "sitting down upon the hill."

The ridicule, I thought, and still think, should be turned the other way. They are the ones to be ridiculed, who shut themselves in behind lath and plaster, and there scrub, sew, and cook, cook, sew, and scrub, scarcely noticing the wondrous show which each season, in turn, prepares for them. Flowers may bloom, trees may wave, brooks may ripple, the whole earth blossom into beauty; but they take no heed. It really does seem like slighting the gifts which God has bestowed.

There is much to admire and to reverence in these women of Tweenit. They are, generally speaking, just as bright and just as good as my friends at Piper's Mills. The point is, that they do not, or the majority of them do not, like those friends of mine, get the *best* out of life. Their energies are spent chiefly on physical, not mental needs. Their talk is trivial. Nature is almost a dead loss to them. While others are enjoying, through books, communion with the noblest minds, they are taken up with the petty concerns of their neighbors. While others seek for knowledge worth the knowing, they are satisfied

to learn that some "Mis Susan" or other has "swapped shawls." And what is true of Tweenit is pretty likely to be true of other places. Then there is another class, not yet considered, the butterfly class, who give their attention chiefly to plumage. Ah, there must be a vast company of women, a multitude whom no man can number, who pick up pebbles, and leave the diamonds!

How is it with the "men-folks," in this respect?

VII.

KINDLING-WOOD.

"LISTENERS never hear any good of themselves." It is really unfair, however, to rank myself in so unworthy a class. No mean listener I, but an earnest inquirer, seeking light on any and every branch of domestic science.

Votaries of the great sciences, it is said, while pursuing their studies with a view to some particular facts or truths, often stumble upon others which are quite as important. And in like manner a few days since, while continuing my observations on the mental status of the women of Tweenit village, did I stumble upon some facts in regard to the opposite sex, which are really worth attending to, and which, at the time, reminded me of the proverb about listeners; for I had the mortification — it was one day when Mrs. Melendy and a few of the neighbors dropped in to help Mrs. Fennel quilt — of hearing man discussed in his capacity of light-wood provider.

"Men-folks" as kindling-splitters! Are husbands, sons, and brothers ready for the question? Have they clear consciences on this point? How many can fearlessly invoke the spirit of free inquiry?

> "And now you're married, you must be good,
> And keep your wife in *kindling-wood*,"

runs the old rhyme. A wise injunction, but one not universally obeyed; that is, if the husbands of Tweenit are representative men in this respect. The heart-rending experiences which were related that day! — the anxieties, perplexities, calamities, agonies! all of which might have been averted by "light wood," as some of them call it.

One *sufferer* took a "sight o' pains" with her cake, "separated" the eggs, "braided" the sugar and butter; but — it fell. Green pine was its ruin. Miss Janet's dumplings "riz right up, light as a feather, the first of it, but came out soggy; and all for lack of a little flash under the pot." Another "had out-of-town company come unexpected one day; and, because there was no light wood on hand to start up a fire in the front-room, they had to sit right down in the kitchen, and see every thing that was going on." Mrs. Melendy's (Mary Melendy's) Dicky was taken ill in the night; and there was an agonizing delay in steeping the "seeny," on account of Mr. Melendy's having forgotten to "split the kindling over night."

And so on, and so on. Men were always apt to forget the kindling, Mrs. Melendy said, but always expected their dinner, *what*ever; and expected light victuals from green pine-wood! Light wood made heavy wood go better. Men didn't understand how tried a woman was with worrying over her fire, and with not having things convenient.

Here the talk diverged, and ran upon things convenient that each would like to have. One wanted a slide-door cut through into the buttery, to save running all the way round with the dishes; another, an oil-carpet, to save washing floor; another, netting in every window and outside door, to save "fighting flies;" another, stationary tubs, with pipes to let the water in and out, such heavy work, lifting tubs! another would have a washer and wringer; another, water let into her sink; and still another wanted her sink-room floor raised up level with the kitchen, it made her back ache so to keep stepping up and down all the time!

And, from things convenient, they went to things pleasant, that "'twould be so nice to have!" Among these were mentioned canary-birds, a melodeon, a magazine, Madame Demorest's Monthly, a set of handsome furniture, lots of pictures, a window built out for keeping plants through the winter, a bathing-room, a set of furs, a whole barrel of lemons and oranges, a lavender-colored poplin dress; and one of the company would like to take a little journey.

I observed that these conveniences and pleasures were spoken of in a jesting, almost sarcastic tone, as if the likelihood of obtaining them were about equal to that of obtaining the crown-jewels of England. In regard to the first, the conveniences, "My husband can't afford it," was a phrase used so often, as to set me to thinking, and that quite seriously. These domestic phrases all have a bearing on my present studies.

"Can't afford it!" Now, it is a question well worth considering, what are the things to be afforded.

In the first place, what is our most precious possession, the best worth having, the best worth saving? Why, life, to be sure! "All that a man hath will he give for his life." "Any thing to save life" is a remark frequently heard.

The next point that I wish to make is, that a woman who overworks sacrifices her life. I have heard women speak of being so tired they could not sleep, but lay all night with "nerves a-trembling," and rose in the morning unrefreshed. Now, no human being can live long in such a condition as that. Well, then, if overwork kills, whatever saves work saves life. Life is the most precious possession: therefore, money spent in saving work is money well spent; and the answer to our question is, that conveniences are the things to be afforded.

But men, that is, many men, do not consider the subject in this light. Apparently, those women were right in saying that a man "don't understand" how "tried" a woman is with not having things convenient. Apparently, men "don't understand" that such words as "backache," "headache," "nervous," "trembling," mean wearing out.

I recollect several cases in which a husband let himself be importuned for some "convenience," week after week, and granted it at last with the bearing of a person doing an inestimable favor; as if he were an outside party, having no interest in the affair at all. I believe, that if Mr. Fennel should provide Mrs. Fennel with "stationary tubs, with pipes to let the water in and out," — tubs, mind, in which to wash his own clothes, — he would consider himself entitled to her everlasting gratitude. At any rate, I see that whenever a washerwoman is hired, the money to pay her comes hard, as hard as lifting the tubs does to Mrs. Fennel and Martha.

I have a friend, who, after his wife really had been injured by bringing water from a well, did at last, by reason of her importunity, put a pump in the sink. And, ever since that great job was accomplished,

whenever she asks for any thing which can possibly be done without, "that pump" serves as an excuse for refusing. Yes, and probably "that pump" will be made to throw cold water on dress, carpet, magazine, or melodeon for many a year to come.

Now, my friend was interested in "that pump" just as much as his wife, only she never had allowed him to find it out. If, when the pailful he brought in the morning — and which he "didn't understand" why it should not last all day — was used up, if then she had let the dinner stop cooking, why, that would have made him "understand." But, instead of doing this, she went to the well herself, knowing that he would "expect his dinner, whatever," to quote Mrs. Melendy.

And observation has shown me that the majority of men, both in Tweenit and out of Tweenit, expect a great deal of women "whatever." They expect a woman will always be good-natured; will keep the whole house in order; will let nothing be wasted; will bear to be found fault with; will never find fault; will have the children look neat; will cook three meals a day; will always have light bread; will wash and iron, make and mend, entertain company, and, if possible, get along without hired help. Yet they do not, as a general thing, exert themselves overmuch to provide her with conveniences, still less with pleasures. Really, this is something like "expecting light victuals from green pine-wood"!

And, now I think of it, I wonder if there be not in the lives of some women too much "green-pine;" if some husbands don't "forget the kindling" all the way through. Mrs. Melendy said that "light wood" would make the heavy wood go better. I wonder if a little "light wood" now and then, in the shape of a pleasure-trip, or of books, music, conveniences, sets of furs, and pretty things in the house, or even of an appreciative or commendatory word, would not make woman's heavy burden of work go better.

VIII.

MR. MCKIMBER RISES TO EXPLAIN.

YES, there is too much "green pine" in the lives of some women; but then, on the other hand, there is equally too much "light wood" in the lives of others. Mrs. Fennel remarked, in the course of the kindling conversation, that sometimes her wood-pile would be all "logs and sog," and next thing 'twould be all "light stuff," and that what you want is to have both together. You want good solid wood to keep the fire agoing; and you want dry pine to make a flash. I gathered from the talk, however, that this ideal wood-pile is seldom found in Tweenit. "If they could all be shaken up together," said Mrs. Melendy, meaning wood-piles, "they would all come out about right." And I suppose it is somewhat so with the lives of women. Some are mostly "green pine;" and some are mostly "light stuff:" if they all could be shaken up together, they all would come out about right.

No concern of mine? Why do I interest myself so much in woman's life and woman's work? Attend to my own affairs? Why, that is just what I am doing. I have discovered from my late course of reading that woman is my "affair." Am I not, as one of the dominant sex, placed in authority over her? Are not her interests in my keeping? Have I not, with others like me, to make the laws which govern her? and to see that she obeys them? and to punish her, if she does not? and to regulate the taxes on her property? and to say what studies she may pursue, and what profession, if any, she may adopt?

And, more than all this, I have, to some degree, the care of her conscience. For instance, if she be doubtful as to the wrongfulness of her rising to speak in prayer-meeting, or in the pulpit, or on the platform, it is my province to decide for her. And, as she is intellectually unable to interpret what the Scriptures have to say on this point, it is my clearer head, as one of the clearer heads of the dominant sex, which must bring out the meaning, and place it where she can see it. And if, after being thus morally and intellectually enlightened, the Spirit move her so strongly, that she must rise and speak, then I, with others in authority, must compel her to silence. Woman? *She* doesn't know what is best for herself. *She* doesn't know, in all cases, right from wrong. Fortunately, she has in man an unerring guide.

My own affairs indeed! It is the affair of all in authority, I should think, to acquaint themselves with the condition of their subjects, in order to legislate wisely, and above all justly. Some of those old Eastern rulers, I believe, used to go among their people in disguise, for this very purpose. Well, so am I a ruler in disguise, acquainting myself with the condition of those over whom I am set in authority; and my disguise is the robe of indifference.

And besides all this, besides being spiritual adviser, instructor, and ruler, I may (though the idea is amusing, and its fulfilment by no means probable), — I may, it is not impossible, be a husband also. And my wife may ask me a question. She will, if she is good; for, if there be one single plain text of Scripture, it is that which bids a woman, if she wants to know any thing, ask her husband at home. And I, for one, mean to take some notice of women, so as to find out beforehand what manner of questions a wife will be likely to ask, lest, not having my answers ready, I be brought to shame. By the way, does not educating women at all rather "go agin that text o' Scripter," to use Mr. David's expression?

Now comes still another consideration, and a very serious one. It is certainly my business to see that woman is fitted for the training of children, because, in this republican country, women's

sons will all help to rule the land. Princes of royal households, it is well known, are cared for from their births with the utmost solicitude. Here every family is a royal household, and every boy is a prince. Every girl is not a princess; but she may become the mother of a prince.

Now, who has the charge of all these royal children at the time when their characters are forming? Who gives the first direction to the minds of those who will in time control the affairs of our country? Woman. And it is my business as an American citizen to learn what are her qualifications for an office of such responsibility.

It was this last consideration which induced me to listen so attentively to my friends at Piper's Mills, and to my friends at the sewing-circle, when the talk ran upon children; for it bore directly on a theory of mine. I suppose every scientist has a theory connected with his science. My theory connected with my science is this: that a mother's chief duty is the taking care of her children. I believe that she should prepare herself solemnly for this duty, and that she should have every possible facility for its performance.

How came I by this theory? I came by it through the newspapers. I never took up one that did not have news to tell of dishonest clerks, corrupt officials, of drunkenness, theft, and murder. And I would say to myself, "Oh, how much badness there is in this dear country! And how do so many people become so bad?"

And one day I went, with my theory upon me, into Mrs. Fennel's kitchen, where I found the women-folk in a state of great consternation. The cakes were all fried for tea; but the salt had been forgotten. "Sprinkle some over them," said I; "'twill strike through, won't it?" "Oh, no!" said Mrs. Fennel. "The salt must be mixed into the dough at the beginning of it."

"There," thought I, "that's the very 'figure of speech' I want! Yes, it comes just right. Let salt stand for goodness, and dough for the children. The goodness must be mixed in at the beginning of it: it is too late when the world has baked the dough up into men and women. It will be of no use then sprinkling it on outside: it won't strike through. All this illustrates my theory exactly. Yes, yes, mix it in at the beginning: that's it! And mothers must do it."

This point being settled, there arise three questions; namely, Is she qualified for this duty? Has she facilities for performing it? Does she feel that it *is* her chief duty?

IX.

"TURN 'EM OFF."

IT was because I had my theory under consideration, — the theory of child-training being the chief duty of a mother, — that I was so much impressed by our neighbor's remark concerning the "three meals." "Now, how is this?" said I to myself. "If 'the three meals take about all day,' and making and mending, the evening, where is the children's time coming from?"

And, indeed, where is it coming from? I see that they get scraps of attention, when, for instance, as in Mrs. Fennel's case, a bit of a sermon is thrown at them now and then in the intervals of cooking, but not often a good square meal. I see that all things else are attended to before the children; not meaning before they are clothed and fed, but before time is taken to talk or read with them. I see that mothers and children are, in a measure, strangers to each other; that they have too little opportunity of becoming intimate. I see, that, with the mothers of Tweenit, life is one prolonged hurry. Feet and hands are hurrying to "get things done." The mind is ever on the stretch, planning how to "get things done," or fearing things will not "get done;" and things do not "get done." One day's work laps over on to the next, one week's on to the next, one month's, one year's; and so there is no pause, no let-down. Rest, quiet, leisure, are here unknown terms with the mother of a family; yet these are just what a mother of a family needs, and must have, for accomplishing what I think is her chief business; for this business of hers requires thought, study, earnest preparation. It requires the mother. Yes, it requires herself personally.

But how shall the children of Tweenit get their mothers, or the mothers their children? No doubt both would enjoy each other's nearer acquaintance. I remember hearing Mrs. Melendy talk one day to her little two or three years old Rosa.

"You 'ittle peshious!" she said. "Mother hasn't had you in her arms to-day. Mother *will* let every thing go, and hold you a *little* while, *whatever!*"

The child was delighted. Both were delighted. They hugged each other. They played peekaboo

They took kisses from each other's lips; and, oh, what a good time they had! It lasted nearly five minutes. Little Rosa would fain have been held longer; but mother had too much to do. The singular part of it was, and the sorrowful part, that Mrs. Melendy appeared to consider her five minutes' good time as a stolen pleasure. It was enjoyed

with the feeling that she ought to be doing something else. I had the curiosity to wait and see what that something else was, and found it to be lemon-pies.

How is my theory going to work in Tweenit, if mothers have to steal time to fondle their children?

I came across a story the other day, which contained an excellent moral, well conveyed. I carried the book in to Mrs. Melendy, and said to her, "This story is exactly the thing for your little boys. You might read it aloud some evening, and talk it over with them."

"O Mr. McKimber!" said she, "if you only knew how much I've got to do! Why, I can't sleep nights thinking of it!"

So there it is again. And how is my theory to work in Tweenit, if boys must go away from home for their amusements, because mothers cannot even steal time to give them?

And how is it to work in other places, and among other classes? I have a cousin living in Elmbridge. She keeps help. I made a little visit there recently, one object of which was to learn whether she does or does not give to her children the leisure thus obtained. She does not. She gives it to extras in the way of cooking, extras in the way of house-adornments, extras in the way of dress. By way of test, I took my book with me, and presented it with remarks like those addressed to Mrs. Melendy on a similar occasion. Her answer was almost identical with that of Mrs. Melendy: "Oh, you don't know how much I have to do!"

And I did not know. I could form no idea of the labor of flouncing that "suit." It had already, she assured me, taken one week's sitting-down time. My theory would not work at Cousin Sallie's. Well, now, thought I, just for the curiosity of the thing, let me try what are called the highest circles. There is one family in the highest circles, the Manchesters, with whom I am on visiting terms. They live in the city. They keep a cook, chambermaid, parlor-girl, nursery-maid, and usually a seamstress. As far as work is concerned, Mrs. Manchester's life is one prolonged state of leisure. Does she give this leisure to her children? She does not: she gives it to society. I thought I would try the "book" in her case, and did so, scarcely able to conceal a smile, as I thought how little she imagined that an experiment was being made upon her for the benefit of domestic science. I said a few words, as on the two former occasions, perhaps enlarging rather more on the desirableness of mothers giving their children more of themselves. But now came in society.

"My dear Mr. McKimber, society demands *so* much! Why, I scarcely have an hour to call my own!"

And I saw that it was so, — saw that what with

shopping, dressing, dinner-parties, evening-parties, callers, and calling, the "chief duty" stood a small chance.

Among all classes, then, — among the wealthy, the comfortably off, and the uncomfortably off, — children are wronged. They are petted, pampered, furbelowed, amused, but still wronged: they are defrauded of their mothers. This is a broad statement; and, of course, there are exceptions. I know myself some thoughtful, careful, prayerful mothers, who understand their mission, and try to fulfil it. But, as a rule, the mission is not recognized. As a rule, children are shoved aside. And this is done in many cases deliberately. Said one of the sewing-circle members, "It won't do to notice your children too much: if you do, you can't turn 'em off."

Yes, "Turn 'em off," is the cry. And turned off they are, — some for "society," some for "flounces," some for "lemon-pies."

How, then, and where, then, is my theory to work? for mothers, exceptions excepted, do not even feel that boy-and-girl-training is their first duty. And, allowing they could be convinced of this, then comes the question of time. How shall they find time to attend to it? which is rather an odd question, as it might be supposed that one's first duty would have the first claim. Ah, well! it is almost a hopeless case. The next generation will not be a good generation, because it will not be started rightly; and it will not be started rightly, because mothers are not attending to their business; and mothers are not attending to their business, because they "have no time," and because they are not aware that it is their business.

Why do not philanthropists organize a society for the enlightenment of mothers? That is what the country needs. And when such a society shall have been organized, and have accomplished its purpose, another must be started, the object of which shall be to furnish mothers with time: not by putting more hours into the day, or more days into the week, but by an easy process which I have in my mind, and which I am willing to divulge. Its name begins with S. I will note down here that the name begins with S.

There is a class of mothers not mentioned in these remarks, who make themselves slaves to their children by trying to gratify all their whims and wishes. This class need enlightenment as much as any other, for the kind of attention which children shall receive is a consideration of the utmost importance.

X.

A LOOK AHEAD.

WHEN the Society for the Enlightenment of Mothers shall have accomplished its work, and, as a consequence, it has become a recognized idea in the community that woman's special duty is to rightly train her children, then it will be in order to organize that other society, the object of which shall be to provide mothers with time for attending to that special duty. And perhaps some of my remote descendants may be called upon to draft resolutions for said society, and may be glad to find, among the musty papers of their great, great, great, many-times-great grandfather, a hint for a beginning, something like this, for instance: —

"*Whereas*, Mothers of families are burdened with many cares, and whereas their crying want is want of time: therefore,

"*Resolved*, That, in our view, the necessities of the age demand the organization of a society, the object of which shall be the diffusion of time among mothers.

"*Resolved, secondly,* That this society boldly takes its stand on the platform of Simplification.

"*Resolved, thirdly,* That, to effectually disseminate its views, this society requires, and shall have, an *organ.*

"*Resolved, fourthly,* That said organ shall be called 'The Columbian Simplifier and Time-Provider;' and that writers shall be pecuniarily encouraged to illustrate in its columns our grand idea of Simplification in its bearing on household duties and on dress."

There, I leave my great, great, great, many-times-great grandchildren these hints, with my blessing, and would leave, also, an article for "The Simplifier," only for the difficulty of putting myself in a frame of mind corresponding with so remotely future a state of things, — a state of things, that is, when the controlling purposes of woman's life shall have changed so entirely.

I have a mind to try to do this, and write my article, and have it read at the sewing-circle; but then it would be premature. These mothers do not yet recognize their mission; neither do they yet place mental culture among the must haves. When they do, they will work for far other than their present aims; not but that many of these are commendable, but that they stand in the way of better things.

Take ironing, for instance. This forenoon I

heard Mrs. Fennel say to Martha, "Don't slight the towels. I take just as much pains with a coarse brown towel as I do with any thing." Mrs. Fennel prides herself on having the clothes "look well on the horse,"* the tinware bright, stove polished, tables scoured, towel-fringes combed out nicely, and a pantry stored with nice things to tempt the appetite. Now, the question is not, are these ends worth attaining, but are they the principal ones worth attaining?

I am aware that any insinuation of this kind read at the sewing-circle would bring a storm about my head at once. "What! slight the ironing?" "What! not scour the tin?" "What! not keep the stove bright?" Well, they would certainly have right on their side; and I should have, more certainly, right on my side. My side being, that, through all the toil and striving, something higher shall be kept in view, and that this something higher shall not be forever shoved aside for those other things lower.

I suppose the Society for the Enlightenment of Mothers will put the case somewhat in this way, —

"As woman has mind, it may be inferred that to

* Clothes-horse, a local term for clothes-frame.

cultivate her mind should be one special object of woman's life. That is one statement. Then, to add another, nothing in the world can be more precious than a little child. It is no light responsibility, that of giving the first direction to an immortal soul. Woman, in assuming a duty so sacred, should feel that its claims rank above all others; that it demands of her her very best.

"A mother, then, should aim at two special duties; namely, to cultivate her mind, and to rightly train her children. Though these two are stated separately, the last really includes the first, since, to rightly train her children, a mother needs to have every mental faculty under cultivation. This implies study, reflection, deliberation; and these imply time. 'We have no time,' say these mothers, — 'no time for books, no time to think, no time to spend with our children.' Which is not true, because they have all the time there is, but feel bound to use it for other purposes."

Now, here is where the Society for the Diffusion of Time among Mothers shall take up the work, and show how, by the application of its grand principle of Simplification to cooking and to dress, the inferior duties can be made to deliver up their "lion's share" of time. Statistical writers in "The

7

Columbian Simplifier" shall state the exact number of rolling-pin strokes required by an average family in a year, and the amount of time said strokes will consume, for the purpose of calculating how many hours and minutes are thus stolen from the two special objects. The same statistical writer, for a similar purpose, shall give, in figures, the stitches and minutes required to flounce an average family for a year. Comic writers will hold up to ridicule, in "The Simplifier," elaborate passages from the cook-book, thus handing them down to posterity, by whom they will be considered as relics of a barbarous age. Among these passages will no doubt be this one concerning

MINCE-PIES.

"Ten pounds of meat, three pounds of suet, one of currants, three of sugar, five of apple, four of raisins, one of citron, a pint of sirup of preserved fruit, a quart of wine, salt, cinnamon, clove, nutmeg, the juice and pulp of a lemon, the rind chopped fine."

Among the illustrations of "The Simplifier" may be, perhaps, one of a woman at a sewing-machine, half-buried in as yet unruffled ruffling; musical instruments at the right of her, an easel with its belongings at the left of her, book-shelves well filled in front of her. If the artist be imaginative, he may depict, hovering over their several emblems, dim, shadowy forms to represent, respectively, the genius of music, of painting, of literature, each vainly, and sorrowfully because vainly, beckoning the ruffler away. Or, instead of a woman ruffling, it may be a woman, chopper in hand, con-

cocting the above-quoted horror of the cook-book, surrounded, of course, by the various ingredients, each properly labelled. If the artist be sensational, as well as imaginative, he may introduce here, instead of the dim and shadowy figures just now mentioned, the grim and shadowy figure of Death as saying with an exultant laugh, "Go on, madam, go on. You are working in my interests!"

Then will come the essayist. Imagine him thus, —

"Some may ask, Mr. Editor, is it not desirable to live neatly, and to cook palatable food? Yes. But is it for this alone that woman has intellect, talent, genius, aspirations? Suppose, now, that one of these women live forty working-years. At the end of that time she can look back, and say, 'I have polished my stove twelve thousand times; have scoured my knives thirty-six thousand times; have never left one wrinkle in one coarse towel; have swept the house from garret to cellar two thousand and eighty times; and I have made unnumbered thousands of cakes, pies, and hot biscuits.' Now, without saying any thing against neatness, or against eating, can that woman, in accomplishing these ends only, be said to have fulfilled the essential purposes of life?

"The case is something like this. A person is sent on an important mission, and, being asked if he has performed his mission, replies, 'Why, no! I had no time. It took all the time to look out for provisions, brush the dust off my clothes, and polish my boots. These duties have been faithfully attended to, I am proud to say.'

"Or suppose a sea-captain should devote his energies mainly to keeping the ship in order and his storeroom supplied, but never steer for any port. '"Cleanliness and good living" is my motto,' he would say, pointing exultingly to his well-scrubbed decks and to his well-filled storeroom. 'Yes; but it is necessary to get somewhere,' might properly be answered.

"Let woman, then, while insisting on neatness, remember her mission. Let her, sailing on life's seas, keep the ship in order and wholesomely provisioned, but at the same time steer for some port."

The essayist will, of course, bring in those who forget their mission while picking flowers, chasing butterflies, and blowing bubbles, and will in various ways show that by simplifying cooking, and simplifying dress, time may be diffused among mothers.

XI.

FENNEL PAYNE AND ADELINE.

TWEENIT is usually in a state of ferment from one cause or another. Last week it was a quarrel between two neighbors; the week before it was Aunt Jinny's (Aunt Jinny under the hill) undertaking to have company; this week, it is silver-plated knives. Fennel Payne has bought for Adeline silver-plated knives. "It does beat all!" exclaims Mrs. Laura, who is now discussing the matter with Mrs. Fennel in an adjoining room. My prophetic eye sees a day in the far-off future, when, even in country villages, women's thoughts will be occupied by subjects of more importance. Meanwhile, Nature abhorring a vacuum, gossip flows in, as one may say, like a sea, filling every little creek and inlet between the solid high lands of housework and needlework.

It is amazing, the relish with which a choice bit of this standard entertainment is enjoyed. Mrs.

Laura comes over on some errand (she is a stoutly-built woman with a determined cast of countenance), and sits down by Mrs. Fennel. The talk begins: it grows interesting. They lean toward each other: there is animation in their faces, a light in their eyes, feeling in every tone. The announcement of a national calamity could hardly be received with greater emotion than is this wonderful news of to-day. "Silver-plated knives? What *do* you mean?"

It was Fennel Payne and Adeline who were criticised by the sewing-circle for their way of spending time and money. Indeed, Tweenit in general disapproves of this couple: it calls them "stuck up." I know this cannot be true of Adeline, because she is an intimate friend of my friend Mrs. Royal of Piper's Mills, and therefore must have common-sense, and therefore cannot be "stuck up." And, as for her husband, I like the looks of him much, and mean to accept his kind invitation to "come over." These two words seem to suffice for all ordinary complimenting in Tweenit, especially at the breaking-up of a gathering, when it fairly rains "come overs." But hark! List! What is Mrs. Laura saying? "Every day!" "They don't keep them for company, but use them every day!"

This is the last straw which breaks the back of forbearance. Purchasing the articles at all was bad enough; but using them "every day" is atrocious. These two, Fennel Payne and Adeline, are rare specimens, which must be examined. The interests of my science demand it. I shall go "over."

TWO WEEKS LATER.

Well, I have been over several times; and I entirely approve of Fennel Payne and Adeline. They are a couple in advance of their times,— a couple worthy to live in the days of "The Columbian Simplifier and Time-Provider." They believe in books, in beauty, in social intercourse, and in out-doors.

I found my friend Mrs. Royal staying there the last time I called. She is quite enthusiastic about Mr. Fennel Payne, and, finding that I sympathize in her enthusiasm, has kindly lent me these extracts, copied from letters which a young friend of hers received from Adeline's sister, one Miss Vining. They eulogize Fennel Payne, and, at the same time, solve the great knife mystery.

EXTRACTS.

. . . "Pretty scenery, river, meadow, woods beyond. They live up stairs, have one cooking-room, one sitting-room, two sleeping-rooms, with garret privileges, and the right to wash in the sink-room, down below, the second pleasant day after Sunday. Adeline does her own work, and takes care of little Adeline and Buddy, as they call baby. He is — but, as the girl in the book says, there never will be a word invented adequate to describe your sister's baby. No, there never will. And such a husband as Adeline has got! Oh, I tell you there are not many Fennel Paynes in this world! Oh, they two do take such comfort! Why, the very atmosphere of the house is full of comfort, and you have to breathe it in.

"Fennel comes home from work at evening, and settles himself down with an air of intense satisfaction, as if this were for him the only spot in all the world. Sometimes he undresses Buddy, Adeline, meanwhile, stepping about, doing up the work, going sideways so as to keep her eyes on them, and telling over all the cunning things baby and little Adeline have committed during the day. At last baby's father, after fumbling at the night-gown strings, and tying them in a single bow-knot, covers him over like a cocoon. Then lullaby, hushaby, softly and gently. Fennel's low tones are wonderfully sweet; and now and then Adeline joins in 'with sweet accord.' I tell you 'tis such a perfect taking comfort, it almost brings the tears to my eyes. That baby's slumbers ought to be sweet, thus watched and tended. But it is so funny to see a man try to glide! In Fennel's tiptoe performances he seems to be putting himself universally out of joint. . . .

"Fennel is unwilling to have Adeline do any very hard work. They live well, but simply; that is,

they have the best of bread, meats, fruit, &c., but no elaborate concoctions which take time to prepare, and cost money to buy. Fennel says he thinks the right way is to save on non-essentials, and spend on essentials. Among essentials he counts books and pictures, especially books that have any bearing on education. He says, that, as Adeline has little Adeline and Buddy to bring up, she ought to have the means of preparing herself to do it, and beautiful things to look at, and leisure to enjoy them, so as to keep herself in a pleasant frame of mind. There is nothing he will not do to make Adeline's work easy for her. I don't mean ever to marry till I find a man just like Fennel Payne. But he has no brother. Alas and alackaday! Why, he even bought silver-plated knives to save Adeline's arms and Adeline's moments. His Aunt Laura was over yesterday; and she gave him quite a lecture on extravagance, also threw out something about the mother of a family sitting down to read in the daytime. Fennel declared that he could buy a set of knives every month with what his aunt spent in cooking the unnecessaries of life; and Adeline did a sum in tarts and doughnuts to show where her reading-time came from. Fennel said, that, if anybody ought to sit down to read in the daytime, it is the mother of a family; for she, more than anybody, needs whatever help books can give. Aunt Laura said she approved of laying by for a rainy day; and Adeline said that was just what she was doing, — laying up ideas against the day when her health might not be so good, or her family so small. 'The question is, Aunt Laura,' said she, 'who wastes time and money, — you, or I?' Uncle David and Aunt Laura have always worked like slaves, and do now; but every dollar saved is put into the bank or into land. There's hardly a pretty thing in their house. They work and save, work and save, denying themselves almost every enjoyment, except that of eating. They will live well. Uncle David owned to Fennel once, that he wants to have the name, when he dies, of leaving property. What a funny idea it is, when you come to think of it, — the idea of living this life, that can't be lived but once, entirely for the sake of accumulating something, which, when we have done living, can be of no use to us! I agree with Fennel and Adeline, that we ought to get out of life what is best worth having. I suppose we can carry that with us; don't you? And I shall not marry until I meet with a man — well, something like Fennel, or, at any rate, who believes as I do in these matters. Though, to be sure, I might take one that differed a little, supposing one offered, and convert him; but it would be advisable to do this last before marriage, perhaps before the engagement. . . .

"Aunt Laura has just come over again, and she and Adeline are discussing the chapel question. They are on opposite sides, of course. 'Tis as good as a play, being in Tweenit now; and I long to stay longer. Such exciting times! The women, it seems, have earned money to build a chapel (there never was any meeting-house here); and now the men, who have all along discouraged them from doing it, they step forward, and want to form a regular parish that shall build the chapel, and run it generally; but they are not going to allow the women to come to the parish-meetings, and speak, — the meetings that are to dispose of their own money, They say it would be wicked. Isn't this funny?" . . .

XII.

NEW INVENTION WANTED.

I HEARD Nanny Joe remark, the other day, that begging money was akin to pulling teeth; and, for her part, she wished there was a way of putting people's avaricious propensities under some influence akin to laughing-gas, that their money might be drawn without pain. I said to her in reply, that fairs answer the purpose very well, as I could testify from experience; having taken them often, and found in every instance the effect to be such, that I scarcely knew of any operation being performed, until I woke up, and found my money extracted. Nanny replied, that such machinery was too cumbersome, and that she meant some little, handy pocket-contrivance to be applied individually. Probably Mr. David was the individual in her mind at the time. The old man is pretty well to do for a farmer; yet his dollars come hard. Every one has roots to it; and the roots are clinched.

Nanny Joe and Nanny Moses have been trying to beg money enough to buy a second-hand sewing-machine for Mrs. Hannah Knowles. Mr. Knowles, a year or two ago, was killed by falling from a roof; and his widow has been struggling ever since to support the family, — yes, struggling, and among all these Christians!

It would seem no more than fair that a home bereft in such a way should be provided with even more comforts than the happier homes around; that a heart thus grief-stricken should be relieved of every possible burden, — no more than fair, and no more than Christian-like. Christianity, it is said, is better than other religions, because it teaches that we are all brothers and sisters. Now, among a family of children, the rule is, when one has any thing good, "Give dear brother or sister some." How often have I heard this at Mrs. Melendy's! And another thing. Yesterday, while I was calling there, little Rosa Melendy fell, and bruised her head. The other children were around her in a moment, — one with a doll, one with a cooky, one with a kiss, one with a flower; all trying to comfort the child. Maybe we are all brothers and sisters, as our religion teaches; but I know that we are not willing, all of us, when we have any thing good, to "give dear brother or sister some," or always eager to heap kindnesses on any member of the family whose heart has been bruised by sorrow.

Nanny Joe says there are very few people — that is, very few people in Tweenit (they are doubtless plenty elsewhere) — who are willing, really willing, to give away half a dollar right out and out. She asked five individuals to contribute that sum toward the sewing-machine, and they refused; they were unmarried men, too, earning daily wages, which were spent freely in tobacco, confectionery, horse-hire, and other gratifications. Nanny says that half a dollar to be spent on one's self is a modest, insignificant little affair; but, if to be given away, it grows so big it can hardly be got out of the pocket.

I wonder how it would be if we all gave, not from pity, or from duty, but, as one may say, impersonally. For instance, I deny myself a pleasure that would cost two dollars, and bestow one costing the same sum upon Mrs. Knowles, saying to myself, "What matters it, since a pleasure is enjoyed, whether the individual Henry McKimber enjoys it, or the individual Hannah Knowles?" This, of course, is merely a hypothetical case.

Mr. David has arrived at no such state of impersonality; neither has Mrs. Laura. I happened to be at their house when Nanny Joe called. Mr. David thought that Hannah Knowles might put out her children, and then go to the almshouse. He said he gave fifty cents three weeks before to help buy a new stove for Aunt Jinny under the hill; also that he felt poorer than common just then, on account of having between one hundred and two hundred dollars not drawing interest, waiting for him to find a safe way of investing it; also that his wife's breaking her arm had been a great damage to him. Nanny Joe offered to accept potatoes, and dispose of them at Piper's Mills. He said potatoes were a cash article, but finally agreed to her taking half a bushel. The tea-table was standing; and I observed that there was no lack of good things to eat. Mr. David, no doubt, takes it for granted that he must have his comforts, whatever others may lack. Perhaps he thinks this is true Bible doctrine. Mr. David is a very doctrinal man.

Nanny Joe asked Mrs. Laura for some old pantaloons to make over for Mrs. Knowles's son. Mrs. Laura replied that her husband and the boys were very hard on their pantaloons. There are two sons at home, Elbridge and Prince, tall, slim *boys* of thirty-five or forty. Elbridge has a small face, and a comical, one-sided twinkle of the eye, which he takes from his father.

Mrs. Laura brought out various garments, in various stages of decay, each of which was examined in turn. One pair would stand it a spell for second-best; another would do for rainy weather; another, for rough work; and so on. A pair of

gray satinets, weak-kneed, and in other respects decrepit, Elbridge remarked, with his one-sided twinkle, were "jest about a herrin'." But his mother declared them to be the very things to wear in the woods. Then he picked up a pair of brown ones, saying they were too short ever to be worn again without "splicing," and that Hannah

Knowles had better take them. His mother said she would see, first, if there were any pieces like them in the bag, "to lengthen the legs down." The bundle-bag was brought forward, roll after roll taken out, and its label read: "Prince's mixed suit o' clothes," "Father's last tail-coat," "Father's summer alpaca waistcoat," "Elbridge's sack cut out by Sally Payne's pattern," "Prince's satinet pantaloons," "Elbridge's frock-coat he had cut out by the tailor," "Elbridge's brown small-legs pantaloons" —

"That's the animal!" cried Elbridge. "But it doesn't look like 'em."

"They'll fade alike, though, some time or other," his mother remarked.

"These won't fade alike, though," he cried, taking up a pair spotted over with paint.

"I've been saving that pair o' pantaloons to braid," answered his mother; "but still" (examining them closely) "they're rather stiff; and on the whole, if Hannah Knowles can make any use of that pair of pantaloons, she may have 'em." "So, Mrs. Laura," thought I, "you give away what is of no use to you. True Bible benevolence that!" Mrs. Laura is a stanch Bible woman.

Nanny Joe declined the generous gift, and rose

to go, fearing, as she afterward told me, that the chapel question might be introduced; which question she had then no leisure for discussing. I came out at the same time, having something to communicate on that very subject. Just as we got outside the gate, a bundle came down plump on the ground in front of us, which same, by unrolling, showed itself to be "Elbridge's brown small-legs pantaloons." We turned, and, guided by a loud *hem*, looked up to the roof, and saw there the comical phiz of the owner protruding from a scuttle. He gave a nod, a finger-shake of warning, and vanished. We picked up the prize, but had a narrow escape with it, as Mrs. Laura opened the door suddenly to ask Nanny Joe if she had seen a certain piece in the paper about woman's sphere.

The dispute as to whether women shall or shall not be allowed to become speaking and voting members of the parish shakes Tweenit to its centre. The sewing-circle members think they should have a voice in the disposal of their own money; but the men, many of them, cannot see their way clear to letting them have a voice in the disposal of their own money, or a voice in their own chapel when it shall be built. The quarrel waxes warm. Not only the neighborhood, but families, are divided. Elbridge

Melendy thinks differently from his father. Martha Fennel and her lover are on opposite sides; and, in their case, the warmth of the argument has produced a coolness of feeling. We shall see what we shall see.

XIII.

A TALK IN THE SCHOOLHOUSE.

AFTER the women, by working at home and begging abroad, had obtained the requisite sum, the men came forward, and proposed meeting together to form a society, or parish, which should build the chapel, and regulate all things pertaining thereto. The women said, "Yes, a very proper thing to do: we'll come." — "Oh, no!" the men said: "we can manage it ourselves. You don't understand house-building; besides, a woman would be out of place in a parish meeting."

Nanny Joe affirmed that she and several members of the sewing-circle had consulted builders, and obtained their proposals. Mr. David answered, very well; that, when the parish should be regularly formed, she could send in a prepared statement, and the parish would act upon it. The matter created quite a stir in the neighborhood; and it soon became evident that Mr. David and others strongly objected to "women speaking in meeting." Some, however, held views opposite to those of Mr. David, and were not backward in expressing those views. At last the direct question was raised, whether, in any future meetings to be held in the chapel, a woman should, or should not, be allowed to speak.

This question has been freely discussed, not upon set occasions, but as people met in their usual way of dropping in; what *he* said, and what *she* said, being told from house to house. Two parties have been formed; and the excitement is very great. Everybody says there was never any thing like it in Tweenit before. There probably was never so much Bible-reading. Each side searches out texts whereby to sustain its position. At first, the women were united; but, latterly, some of them, influenced by husbands, brothers, or lovers, have come out against themselves. Mrs. Laura says she has said, "Amen!" or "Glory!" occasionally in a revival-meeting at Piper's Mills, but that was before she looked into the subject; and she sees now, that, as the command forbids women to speak, one word is as wrong as twenty words. Mr. David and others say that the text is plain and direct, and therefore they cannot conscientiously worship in the building, if women speak in the meetings. The opposite party contend that the prohibition was a local affair, applying only to the women of those days, and of that Eastern country. Mr. David replies, that, if you are going to explain away the Bible, you may as well not have any Bible.

Fennel Payne and some others propose that the men meet in the schoolhouse, and there talk the matter over, and, if possible, come to some decision. Mr. David says he is ready to do this, if Fennel Payne's party will take the Bible literally, and not add, nor take away, nor explain away.

Four days later. Last evening the men came together in the schoolhouse. Those who live near brought lamps, candles, and lanterns, which, being set in a row on the desk, did their best to bring out the low ceiling and dingy walls. Mr. David opened the discussion by saying that he saw no reason for any discussion at all, if we believed the Bible; for there was the text in plain words: "*It is not permitted that a woman should speak in the church.*"

Fennel Payne asked whether the word "church" meant a building, or the collection of people who partake of the sacrament, and are called "the church." Mr. David said it probably meant either, or both. "Then," said Fennel, "if a collection of people who do not belong to the church assemble in a building which is not a church, a woman may speak to them?"

Mr. David began to say that the prohibition was probably intended to cover — but Fennel reminded him that nothing was to be added, or subtracted, or explained away.

Then a man named Hale rose, and asked if it were right for women to teach in sabbath schools. "Certainly it is!" answered Mr. Zenas Melendy, "very right and very proper." — "And if," continued Mr. Hale, "inquirers anxious for the welfare of their souls should come to your wife, seeking light on religious subjects, it would be right for her to give them information?" — "Certainly!" answered Mr. Zenas. "She would be very blameworthy in not doing it." — "On the contrary," replied Mr. Hale, opening his Testament, "she is strictly forbidden to do it. Here Paul says, '*I suffer not a woman to teach.*' This excludes women from teaching the truths of the gospel, from teaching in the sabbath school, in high schools, normal schools, any schools."

"But Paul didn't mean," began Mr. Zenas — "Excuse me," interrupted Mr. Hale. "The conditions are, not to add, nor subtract, nor explain away. And here in Ephesians is another text."

Mr. Hale then read, "*Wives, submit yourselves to your husbands in every thing,*" and asked if that command were to be obeyed without adding, subtracting, or explaining away.

"Why, yes," answered Mr. Zenas, with a hesitancy which caused a general smile; it being pretty well understood in Tweenit that Mrs. Zenas does not fulfil that command to the very letter.

"This injunction, then," remarked Mr. Hale, "takes from wives all personal responsibility. Submit yourselves to your husbands in *every thing.* If a husband wishes his wife to do a wrong act, it is her duty to obey him."

Mr. David said, that, of course, a woman should not do any thing against her own conscience. Mr. Hale replied, that the text left her no right of private judgment, inasmuch as Paul declared over and over again in his epistles, that the wife must submit to the husband, and that "*the husband is the head of the wife, as Christ is the head of the church.*" "And here," Mr. Hale continued, "is a passage which commands us to '*Owe no man any thing.*' Those who cannot worship in a building in which women speak cannot worship with any person who is in debt. And here again" (turning the leaves) "are other texts: '*Let no man seek his own, but every man another's wealth.' 'Bear ye one another's burdens.'* These are equally emphatic: if one binds, all bind."

It was at this point that Cyrus Fennel (brother of Martha) made a hit at Mr. David. He arose, and, looking toward the old man, said he should like to inquire whether Christ's commands were as binding as those of Paul? Mr. David said that certainly they were, and more so. Cyrus then read these words of Christ: "*Give to every man that asketh of thee.*" This brought to every face an amused, half-pleased expression; Mr. David's stinginess being almost a by-word here. He replied, that every man has a duty to his family. Fennel Payne reminded him again that nothing was to be explained away, and then read other commands of Christ, each of a similar import to the one mentioned by Cyrus. He then repeated all the different texts which had been brought forward, beginning with that against women speaking in the church. "And now I want to ask," he continued, "why the first of these injunctions should be taken literally, and the others not?"

As Fennel Payne sat down, a tall, gray-haired man arose, — the same who came through the place, not long ago, selling "Bitters" of his own making.

He is a pleasant-faced, good-humored man, and travels, with his jugs, in an antique carryall, on the outside of which is written with chalk, "Archangel Bitters." His name is Hensiford. This man arose, and, after asking permission to speak, said in a bland, mild tone, speaking slowly, "My friends, it comes to my mind to ask a question, which is this: Why are men met together to decide this matter? My friends, if the Almighty Creator meant that woman should be judged by the law, he gave to her an understanding mind to understand the law: otherwise, God is unjust. And, my friends, if women are to be saved, or lost, according to the deeds done in the body, it must be that they have consciences whereby they may tell right from wrong: otherwise, God is unjust. My friends, woman either is a responsible being, or she is not a responsible being: she can't be sometimes one, and sometimes the other. It does not appear to me, my friends, that we are called upon to decide this matter. The brother on my right hand allowed, just now, that woman should be guided by her conscience. Paul asks, 'Why is my liberty judged of another man's conscience?' Women might ask the same question by putting in the word 'any' in place of 'another.' And now, my friends," continued the old man, looking round with a persuasive smile, "what a plain and simple way it would be to let women understand *Scripter* with their own understandings, and regulate their behavior by the voice of their own consciences!"

XIV.

AN ENTERTAINING MEETING.

THE great chapel question has been decided at last by a *coup d'état*. Cyrus Fennel had promised to give a lot of land; and the deed was made out some time ago, but not signed. At last, growing impatient with what he called the narrowness of Mr. David and a few others, Cyrus declared that he never would sign the deed, unless it was agreed that any person and every person who might feel moved to speak in their meetings should have liberty to do so. Some one suggested to Mr. David that he come up with Cyrus by giving a lot of land himself. This thunder-clap of a suggestion cleared Mr. David's mental vision sufficiently to enable him to perceive that the minority should not stand out longer against the majority, and that possibly, by entering their protest, they had done all that was required of them.

Previous to this, however, a plan was proposed,

which elicited a curious little bit of information in regard to the law. The plan was, that the sewing-circle should build and own the chapel. Some one queried whether or not this could be done legally; and, to make sure, Mrs. Hale and Adeline Payne went to Elmbridge one day, and consulted a lawyer.

The sewing-circle met here that afternoon; and, on returning from Elmbridge, the two delegates hastened over to announce the result of their mission. The lawyer had assured them, they said, that no company of married women could own a building, or any other property. "Not even a hen-house," said Adeline. "The lawyer told us, that, if we two should want to set up storekeeping together, we couldn't own our stock of goods."

This announcement was followed by a dead calm, and the dead calm by a hurricane of exclamations: "Well, I declare!" "Now, if that isn't a good one!" "What, not when we earned the money to build it?" "Pretty state of things!" "I don't see why not!" "The ones that made that law better make it over!" *

There was an old lady present, — a frequent visitor in Tweenit, — one Mrs. Heath, commonly called

* Recent legislative proceedings show that some law-makers are of the same opinion.

"Aunt Mary," a white-haired, sallow-faced, but, on the whole, a pleasant-looking old lady. When the storm had subsided, Aunt Mary remarked in her quiet way, that she could tell them a fact or two about law. Her fact or two was as follows. She married, at the age of twenty-six, a seafaring man five years older than herself. Her husband made only one voyage after they were married. He owned a house and a small piece of ground: another piece was bought, partly with her money, both together making quite a snug little farm. She kept boarders some of the time, and made a practice of taking in work (tailoring had been her trade) in order to help along, so that what money was raised from the place might be spent on the place. They had no children. After twenty-eight years of married life she became a widow. The law gave her one-half the personal property, and the improvement of one-third of the real estate: the rest went to her husband's brother. "A share of the place was set off to me," said Aunt Mary, "and rights of way 'allowed me' across my own premises. I had some privileges in the house too, besides the rooms that were set off to me; the privilege, for instance, of going through my own front entry, and into my own sinkroom. Every thing in the house was appraised. Samuel took half of the furniture, dishes, beds, and bedding; took some things made of inlaid work and of shell-work, — things I set a good deal o' store by, because my husband brought them home to me before we were married. Li-zy kind o' hated to take 'em; but she said, says she, 'You know everybody likes to have what's their own.'"

"Couldn't he have made a will?" asked some one.

"Oh, yes! he could, and he did mean to make one. I was only speaking of the law. He meant to give it all to me."

While Aunt Mary was telling her story, old Mr. Hale came in, father to the Mr. Hale who spoke in the meeting. The old man said he couldn't help feeling an interest to know how the lawyers laid down the law.

After hearing the decision, and hearing Aunt Mary's story, he said, "Wal, ladies, you woman-kind must make up your minds to let patience have her parfect work. The laws favor ye more than they did. Women have come up considerable since Paul's day. I don't believe there's a minister in the land would stand up and preach a discourse in favor of that text, 'Women, submit yourselves unto your husbands in every thing.' He'd be laughed down. And suppose a writer should write an es-*say* to prove that wives ought to keep that command, and send it to that biggest New-York double newspaper. What would the editor do with that es-*say?* Put it into his head column?

"You jest wait. There's a great to-do now about a woman's gittin' up to speak in a revival-meetin'. Wal, in my father's day, there was a great to-do about their not wearin' their veils into the meetin'-house. Ministers took sides, and arter a while it got into the Boston newspapers. The greatest ministers in the State preached for and agin it. There was a famous minister came to our town. I've heard my father tell the story many a time. Father said he was among the last of his teens then, and said he used to sit in a square pew in the gallery, back to the pulpit; and the girl he wanted to go with sat down below, jest far enough off, and not too near, for him to keep lookin' at her, and she at him, now and then; and that kind o' took up his mind in sermon-time. He had never durst to try to be her beau in earnest. He'd walked alongside once or twice, but never'd had the face to offer his arm; and he'd made dependence on his Sundays, and been steady to meetin' for reasons aforesaid. Wal, when the veil question begun to make a stir, all the girls, and she among 'em, became persuaded in their minds they ought to wear their veils into the meetin'-house, and keep 'em down; and this caused a dreadful *de*privation to him, and to others likewise.

"And, arter things had gone on so a spell, there came a famous preacher to town, one of the uncommon rare ones; and he preached a sermon with thirteen heads, all goin' to show that women could keep their veils down, or not keep 'em down, jest as they pleased. That was in the forenoon. Father said, that, in the arternoon, every single girl in that meetin'-house sat all meetin'-time with her veil up. He said 'twas jest like light breakin' in arter a cloudy shadow."

"And what about the girl?" asked Martha Fennel. "Did he have the girl?"

"No. The girl had a young man that she didn't look at, that sat over across in the other gallery."

"But it can't be true," remarked Adeline Payne, "that ministers really did pretend to dictate whether women should wear veils, or not?"

"Jest what Mr. Picket's wife said, over at Elm Bridge, when I told them this same story. I said 'twas actooally true. And Mr. Picket, said he, 'I tell you how we'll prove it. You said 'twas in the old Boston newspapers. My cousin goes representative to General Court. They keep files of the old Boston papers in the Boston Library,' says he; 'and I'll write my cousin word to look 'em over.' We reckoned back, and found father must have been among the last of his teens about the year 1800. So Mr. Picket wrote word to his cousin; and his cousin looked the files over, and found a paper that had a piece in it on this very subject; and the name of the paper, if I don't mistake my memory, was 'The Columbia Sentinel.'"

I was quite interested in this little story of Mr. Hale's. Indeed, since my attention has been called to domestic science, I have felt a steadily-increasing interest in whatever relates to the condition of women, past, present, and future. Previous to that, I used to think, or rather took it for granted in an indifferent way without thinking, that, in matters of religion, women were on an equality with men. I had the impression that this equality was claimed for one of the results of Christianity as being enjoined by the text, ending, "Neither male nor female, but all one in Christ Jesus." A few sarcastic remarks of Nanny Joe (which remarks I had in mind while writing one of the early numbers of these papers), together with some of my own observations, have caused me to read with close attention the discussions which are so continually going on in the papers in regard to what woman should or should not be allowed to do. And, with all my reading and all my thinking, I can arrive at no other conclusion than that of my friend who sells "Archangel Bitters;" namely, that woman, having been endowed by her Creator with mind and with conscience, should be left to understand Scripture with her own understanding, and to judge for herself what is right, and what is wrong, man not being accountable therefor.

XV.

THE WRITER FACES HIS OWN MUSIC.

A LADY-FRIEND, after looking over my papers, asked why I harped so much on the rather low and trivial subject of eating. "Because," said I, "daily observation has driven me to it." And this is just the truth. I see that everybody takes it for granted they must have good living, "whatever," to use Mrs. Melendy's word, rather than pleasures of a higher grade, even the pleasure of helping the needy.

Take a close-fisted man like Mr. David, who, though well enough off, practises the strictest stinginess. With him the spending of each dime is carefully considered. A half-dollar given away is, as one may say, hung up in his memory, set in a frame, for handy reference. When such a man affords his family cakes, pies, preserves, and the like, for their daily food, we may consider such things to be firmly established as "must haves."

Indeed, all classes, poor as well as rich, seem to agree that the earning and compounding of these and similar articles rank among the chief objects of life. The very phrase "good living" shows this, since it implies that to live well is to eat well. A man said to me the other day, "When I can't eat and drink what I want to, then I want to die."

Now, if we were created only a *little* lower than the angels, there certainly should be a wider space between us and the inferior animals than such a state of gormandism denotes. Not that the pleasures of eating are to be wholly despised. There is, after all, a relationship between us and the brutes; and we need not be ashamed to own our kindred, or to share in their enjoyments. Besides, these grains, fruits, vegetables, &c., which we are called to meet three times a day, are all our relations, on the mother's side (Mother Nature's), and should by no means be regarded with contempt, especially as it is their destiny to be worked up into human beings, actually made bone of our bone, and flesh of our flesh.

I believe in festival days with all my heart, which is the very best way of believing. I think we should sometimes call our friends together, and gratify the whole of them (not meaning all of them, but the whole nature of each one), — give them bright thoughts for the intellect, friendliness for the heart, and good things for the palate, keeping, as regards the last, within the bounds of common-sense and healthfulness.

The palate craves enjoyment; and that craving, being a natural one, must be recognized as such. But what I insist upon is this; namely, that gratifying the palate shall not rank among the chief occupations or the chief enjoyments of life, for it has usurped those positions long enough.

And not only is it an usurper, crowding out better and more ennobling aims, but it makes slaves of women, and seriously affects their peace of mind. I have a bright-eyed young cousin, whose one idea, during the first half of the day at least, is to prepare a dinner which shall please the fastidious taste of her husband. For this end she works, plans, ponders, experiments, contrives, invents, and consults cook-books and cooks; and, this end attained, she is happy. But I have seen her at mealtime, when he has criticised unfavorably a dish on which she had spent much labor and more anxiety, — have seen her flush up, leave the table on some pretended errand, and (this is actual truth) brush tears from those bright eyes of hers. Another case. An elderly woman of this village died recently, the chief end and aim of whose whole married life had been, so people say who know, to cook in such a manner as exactly to please her husband. She succeeded. That husband made the remark, in this very house, and within this very week, that he hadn't tasted a decent piece of custard-pie since his wife died. Among the wealthier classes it is just the same. I believe that Mrs. Manchester goes to her dinner-table every day with fear and trembling. Perhaps her case is worse than that of my cousin, as, with Mrs. Manchester, success or failure depends on the uncertain capabilities of Irish help. The blame, however, if blame there be, rests on Mrs. Manchester; and I have seen that the sarcastic manner in which Mr. Manchester blames, sometimes cuts into the quick. These may be exceptional cases: I trust they are. But that this state of things does prevail more or less generally, cannot be denied. If, then, the low and trivial matter of eating be sufficiently high and important to take so very prominent a position among our enjoyments, and to seriously affect the peace and happiness of woman's life, why not harp on it?

It should be harped on, likewise, because it affects the condition of almost everybody. Simplify cookery, thus reducing the cost of living, and how many longing individuals, now forbidden, would thereby be enabled to afford themselves the pleasures of culture, of travel, of social intercourse, of tasteful dwellings! And it might be added, at the risk of raising a smile, how many pairs of waiting lovers, now forbidden, would thereby be enabled to marry, and go to—paradise, which is to say housekeeping!

Social intercourse, in a special manner, would be affected by the change. People "can't have company, 'tis such hard work!" And no wonder! A young woman of this village set before her company, the other afternoon, three kinds of cake, two of pie, three of preserves, besides Washington-pie, cookies, and hot and cold bread. Every woman who sat at that tea-table, when her turn of inviting the company comes round, will feel obliged to make a similar display. When this barbarous practice of stuffing one's guests shall have been abolished, a social gathering will not necessarily imply hard labor and dyspepsia. Perhaps, when that time arrives, we shall be sufficiently civilized to demand pleasures of a higher sort. True, the entertainments will then, in one sense, be more costly, as culture is harder to come by than cake. The profusion of viands now heaped upon the table betrays poverty of the worst sort. Having nothing better to offer, we offer victuals; and this we do with something of that complacent, satisfied air with which some more northern tribes present their tidbits of whale and walrus.

When we have changed all this, it will then be given us to know the real pleasure of eating. At present our appetites are so vitiated by over-eating, that the keen edge of this pleasure is dulled. Whoever would enjoy it, sharpened at both edges, let him labor hard enough to feel actual hunger, and then take—why, take any simple thing, a baked potato, a slice of meat, a piece of bread. The dishes that make the work, and cost the money, are usually eaten after hunger is satisfied, and do harm, rather than good.

We often hear people remark, "Oh! we don't want to be thinking of what does harm, and what does good. The best way is to eat what's on the table." I know a mother who gives her only child, a little girl three years old, hot biscuits, mince-pie, rich cake, and the like, believing, she says, that "a child's stomach should get used to every thing." For her part, she believes in living the natural way, not in picking and choosing. Why not, on the same principle, let the child get used to all kinds of reading, and all kinds of companions?

It is curious, the way people assume, that, because the present system of cooking and serving meals is customary, it is, therefore, natural; as if the courses of a dinner, each with its central dish, and that with its revolving lesser dishes, were, equally with the solar system, an established order of nature. Meal-providers have sought out many inventions, and call these the "natural way." They give us, at one sitting, fish, pork, flour, butter, salt, milk, eggs, raisins, spices, corn, potatoes, squash, coffee, sugar, saleratus, pickles, onions, lard, pepper, cooked fruits, tomatoes, essences, all variously combined, and say, "Here, eat, eat in the natural way." Why natural? The men and women it helps to produce are, to some extent, its natural consequences; but are they natural men and women? Hear them. "Oh, my head!" "Oh, my back!" "Oh, my side!" "Oh, my liver!" "Oh, my stomach!" "Oh, my nerves!" On every side resounds the mournful chorus. Seldom do we hear break in even one jubilant voice, chanting in response, "I am in perfect health. I feel no ache, no pain." Is this, then, the natural way? But the system speaks for itself, or, rather, the innumerable host of invalids speak for it. So does the grand army of doctors. So do proprietors of patent medicines, rolling in wealth. Why, people take ill health for granted. "No use telling your aches: everybody has 'em," is a remark often heard.

Occasionally an individual rebels, and insists on eating really simple and natural food. Such individual is straightway called odd. He is jeered at, ridiculed, accused of thinking about his stomach, and about what merely goes to sustain the body, as if such thinking were not worth while.

Now, these bodies are nearer and dearer to us than any other earthly possession. And, what is more, they will cling to us. We are joined to them for better or worse; and from this union there is no divorce, till death do us part. Why, then, scoff at them? Why not, on the contrary, seriously consider how we may build them up as pure, as strong, and as perfect as may be? Not worth while to think about one's stomach? Why? The stomach is not an obscure party, doing business in a small way, and on its own account. It is leading partner in an important and influential firm, — "Stomach, Brains, & Co." There is nothing vulgar about brains; oh, no! They have always been respectable. Well, in this great firm, each member is liable for all, and all for each. If one runs in debt, the others have to pay. It is well known that the condition of the brain and other organs is affected by the quality of the blood, and the quality of the blood, by the quality of the food. The change of food into blood is a chemical process; and why is not human chemistry as well worth studying as any other kind? for instance, that by which the manufacturer selects the best chemicals for his various dyestuffs, and the gardener those best adapted to his various soils. The time may come when this chemistry of eating shall rank with other scientific studies. People shall then be allowed to "pick and choose" the diet best calculated to make healthy nerves, blood, bones, &c.; and they shall not suffer ridicule for so doing.

www.ingramcontent.com/pod-product-compliance
Lightning Source LLC
LaVergne TN
LVHW021426110826
845150LV00007B/2103